Bo and the Witch

Read more UNICORN DIARIES books!

Unicorn Diaries

Bo and the Witch

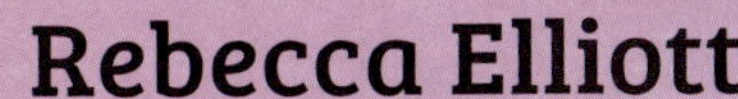
Rebecca Elliott

For Rosie and Lily, with love. XX —R.E.

Special thanks to Clare Wilson
for her contributions to this book.

Library of Congress Cataloging-in-Publication Data

Names: Elliott, Rebecca, author, illustrator. | Elliott, Rebecca. Unicorn diaries ; 10.
Title: Bo and the witch / Rebecca Elliott.
Description: First edition. | New York : Branches/Scholastic, 2024. |
Series: Unicorn diaries ; 10 | Audience: Ages 5-7. | Audience: Grades K-1. |
Summary: When Charm, a young witch, crash-lands in Sparklegrove Forest, Bo and the other young unicorns set out to help her with her flying skills and her confidence.
Subjects: LCSH: Unicorns—Juvenile fiction. | WitchesJuvenile fiction. | Magic—Juvenile fiction. | Self-confidence—Juvenile fiction. | Helping behavior—Juvenile fiction. | Diaries—Juvenile fiction. | CYAC: Unicorns—Fiction. | Witches—Fiction | Magic—Fiction. | Self-confidence—Fiction. | Helpfulness—Fiction. | Diaries—Fiction. |
BISAC: JUVENILE FICTION / Readers / Chapter Books | JUVENILE FICTION / Animals / Dragons, Unicorns & Mythical | LCGFT: Diary fiction.
Classification: LCC PZ7.E45812 Blk 2024 | DDC [Fic] —dc23
LC record available at https://lccn.loc.gov/2023039184

ISBN 978-93-5954-057-3

10 9 8 7 6 5 4 3 2 1 24 25 26 27 28

Printed in India at Sai Printo Pack Pvt. Ltd.
First edition, June 2024
This reprint edition, June 2024
Illustrated by Rebecca Elliott

Edited by Cindy Kim
Book design by Marissa Asuncion

Table of Contents

Sunday

Hi, Diary! It's me, Rainbow Tinseltail, but you can call me Bo.

Sorry if my writing is a bit wobbly. I keep looking up at the sky instead of at the page! You see, witches learn to fly at this time of year. I don't want to miss them!

I live in Sparklegrove Forest. Lots of magical creatures live here.

Witchester School

Snowbelle Mountain

Unipods

Fairy Village

Goldie's Cave

Twinkleplop Lagoon

Goblin Castle

Some live high up in the clouds – like witches!

Here's what I know about witches:

Witches fly above the clouds. They're hard to spot because they don't come down to the ground.

They're also great at spells and potions.

Cauldron

Most witches have a special pet that travels with them.

Their broomsticks leave behind sparkly streaks in the sky.

Most unicorns can't fly. But some unicorns can, like my friend Nutmeg. Here are some facts about <u>all</u> unicorns:

Want to know more about us?

We like to paint pictures with our horns.

When we use our powers, magical stars twinkle around us.

Unicorns aren't born. Instead, we appear on very starry nights.

A ladybug landing on our horn brings us good luck.

We don't have parents. Our friends are our family! My friends and I go to Sparklegrove School for Unicorns (S.S.U.). We live together in **UNIPODS.**

We all have different Unicorn Powers. I'm a Wish Unicorn, so I can grant one wish every week. My best friend Sunny can turn invisible!

Here is my teacher and all my other unicorn friends with their magical powers.

At school, we study **SPARKLE-TASTIC** subjects like:

MAGICAL MIME

SKY-GAZING

FORTUNE-TELLING

THE POWER OF FRIENDSHIP

We all have a special unicorn patch blanket. We learn something new every week to earn our next patch.

I should get ready for sleep now, Diary. I need to get up early tomorrow to do some more witch-spotting! Sleep well!

2
A Charming Witch

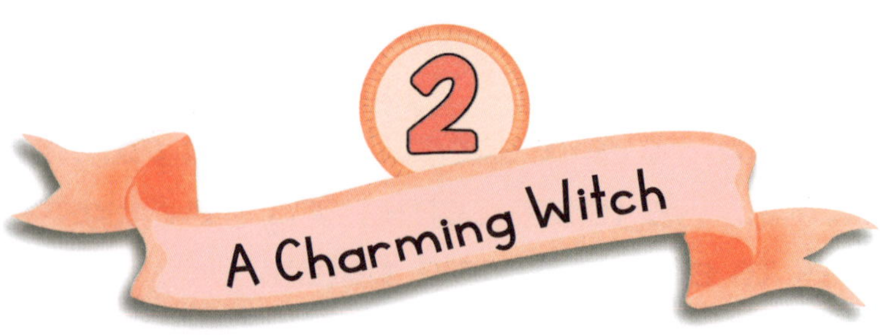

Monday

After our lessons this morning, Mr. Rumptwinkle took us to Budbloom Meadow to look for witches.

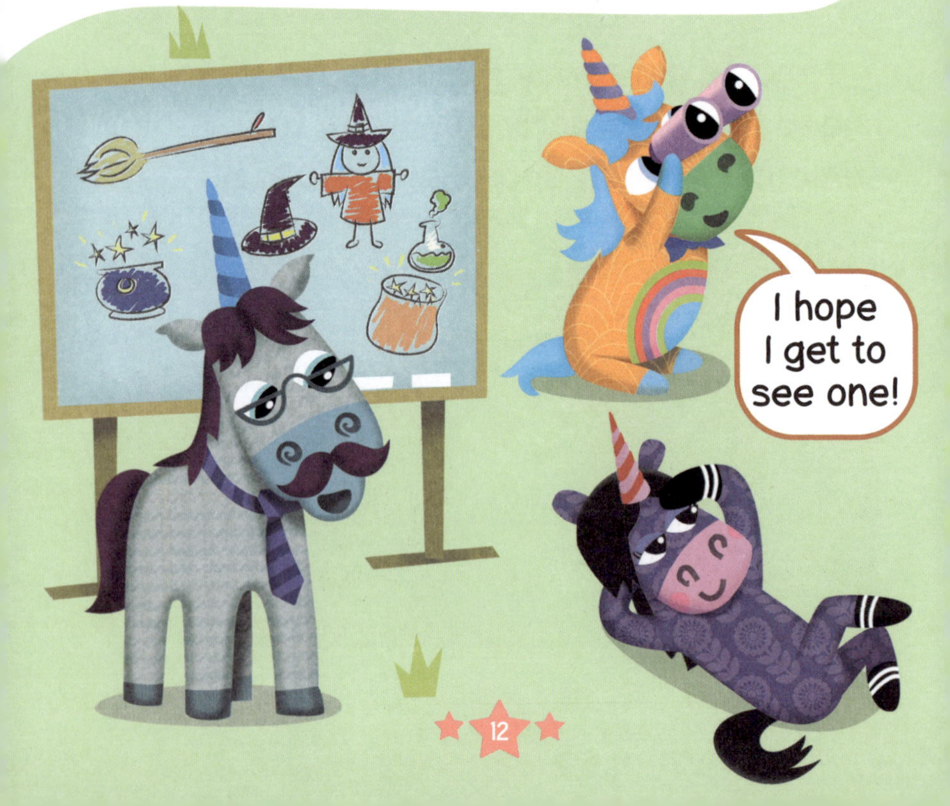
I hope I get to see one!

Me too! They leave swirling streaks in the sky.
Since you fly, you must see witches all the time, Nutmeg!
Well, actually, I can't fly above the clouds. So this is the only time I get to see them, too!

We sky-gazed all afternoon. We saw beautiful clouds and a family of tree sprites. But there were no witches.

With no luck, most of the class decided to leave. But Mr. Rumptwinkle let Nutmeg, Piper, Sunny, and me stay behind.

After we sat for a while, Sunny suddenly jumped up!

We quickly galloped over to the witch. She had landed in a soft pile of leaves.

We held on to the witch's feet and pulled her out.

Oh my, I fell far! Thank you, unicorns!

Hello, my name is Charm.

Hi, I'm Bo! This is Sunny, Piper, and Nutmeg.

We couldn't believe we were talking to an actual witch!

Wow, that was a big fall!
Yes, I crashed because . . . well, some birds flew in front of me.
Can you help me find my broom?
Of course we can!

The four of us dived into the leaves.

We held up what we each thought was the broom. But . . .

Your broom is broken!
Oh, FLAMING CAULDRONS! That's not good!
Can you fix it with a spell?
No. For this broom to fly, we would need to make a flying potion. But I would need a witch's cauldron for that.

Oh dear. Do you want to come back to our unipods? We can come up with a plan.

That would be amazing! As a thank-you, I'd love to bake something for you all.

That sounds great!

On the way back home, Charm picked sugar plums and **TWINKLEBERRIES**.

Soon, we were at the **UNIPODS**. Mr. Rumptwinkle, Monty, Scarlett, and Jed couldn't believe their eyes. It was a real witch!

Hi, I'm Charm!

Hello! This is Jed, Scarlett, and Monty, and I'm Mr. . . . um –

Mr. Rumptwinkle!

Yes, that's right!

We told Mr. Rumptwinkle and the others how Charm had made a crash landing. And everyone agreed that Charm should stay for as long as she needed.

So Charm happily started baking. She baked the most YUMMY cupcakes.

As we were eating, Monty got a bit curious.

So, what made you crash your broom?

Oh, um . . . a big gust of wind, I think?

A bit earlier, Charm had said that birds had made her crash. I wondered why she was giving a different reason now. But I guess that doesn't really matter.

We chatted and giggled with Charm for hours. What an amazing day, Diary! We have a new friend, and she's a witch!

3
A Magical Feather

Tuesday

At breakfast this morning, we ate **TWINKLE-TASTIC TWINKLEBERRY** pancakes that Charm made.

Oh, please use one of mine!

Thank you, Nutmeg, I was hoping you'd say that!

Yay! Let's make Charm a new broom!

Charm started teaching us what to do.

Mr. Rumptwinkle trotted over, and we told him about our plan.

I love how you're learning from one another. So, unicorns, this week, you can try to earn your Learning Patch. Charm might even learn some things from you all, too!

Charm wrote us a list of everything we needed.

Magic Broomstick Materials

- One bag of fairy dust
- Willow branches
- Dandelion stalks
- Magical meadow grass
- Twigs from twenty different trees
- Reeds from Rainbow Falls

Then we split up to find the materials in the forest.

I quickly found fairy dust.

When we returned, Charm taught us how to weave together the bottom of the broom.

While we worked, she told us that she goes to Witchester School. We asked what she learns there.

It's mostly potions, spells, fortune-telling, and broom flying. Oh, and math.

Wow, I bet you're good at all of it!

Before Charm could answer, Nutmeg threw herself on the ground.

Okay, I'm ready to give up one of my feathers – be gentle!

Nutmeg, you're so kind to do this.

Oh, this is no big deal!

Piper gently plucked out one of Nutmeg's feathers while we all made funny faces.

Nutmeg flew up and twirled in the sky.

And I can still fly okay!

That's better than okay – you're amazing!

Your broom is ready now, Charm!
Can you show us how amazing your flying is?

Charm sat on her new broom. I was so excited to see her fly!

But then she got right back off!

At **CLOUDTIME**, Charm made us all a delicious mug of **HOT CHOCO-MYSTIC**.

Yummy!

You're SO good at making tasty food and drinks, Charm!

Thank you! I love baking and cooking!

I was glad Charm was still staying with us. But something didn't seem right.

Does it seem strange that Charm didn't fly home today?

Yeah, I guess so. But it *was* getting dark. And she was probably tired. There's always tomorrow!

Well, Diary, Sunny is right, there is always tomorrow!

4 The Worst Witch

Wednesday

The smell of sugar plum muffins woke us up early this morning. YUM!

Wow, delicious! Thank you SO much!

You're very welcome!

After breakfast, we can't wait to see you fly!

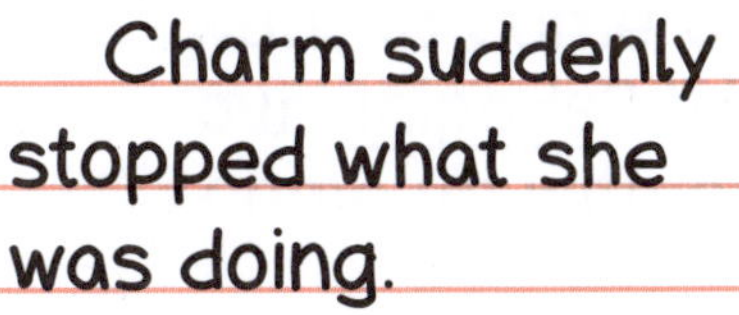

Charm suddenly stopped what she was doing.

Um, there's something I haven't told you.

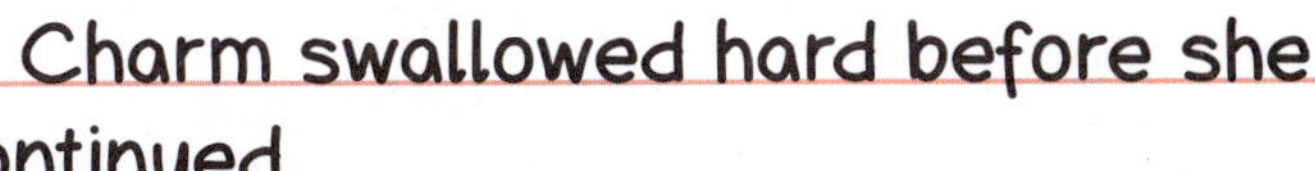

Charm swallowed hard before she continued.

I'm not very good at flying. In fact, even though I have a lovely new broom, I'm not sure I can fly home.

I'm sure you're not that bad.

Oh, I am. I'm the worst witch in all my classes. The only thing I'm good at is baking! And, well, that's not a very witchy thing to do.

We all felt sorry for Charm.

Well, we think you're the best witch ever!
And I'm sure you're better at magic than you think.
Thank you. But watch me try to turn this pumpkin into a mouse.

Charm scrunched her eyes tight and raised her hands toward the pumpkin.

Suddenly, a cloud of sparkles burst around the pumpkin. The pumpkin magically turned into . . . a banana!

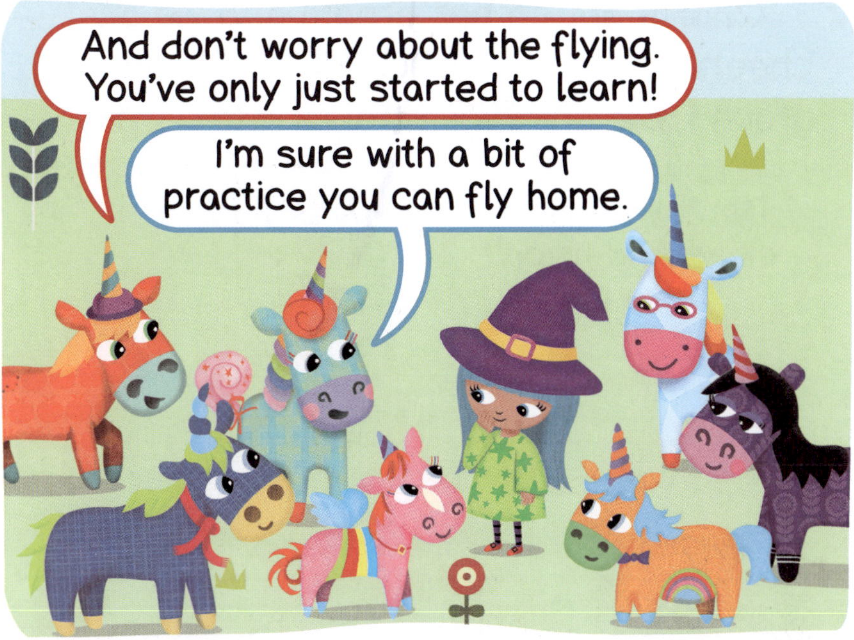

And don't worry about the flying. You've only just started to learn!

I'm sure with a bit of practice you can fly home.

Charm smiled.

Charm got on her broom and we all cheered as she WHOOSHED off the ground. But she flew straight into a tree!

She mounted her broom and shot off in the opposite direction.

Sunny, Nutmeg, and I galloped to **TWINKLEPLOP LAGOON** just as Charm splash-landed into it!

Charm smiled before taking off again.

We caught up to her just as she flew upside down through a fairy parade.

We looked up to find Charm.

She flew in loop-the-loops over and over again until she sped forward . . . and crashed right into a dragon!

Well, hello there, little witch!
Sorry!
That's okay! It looks like you're new to flying.
Nutmeg is the best flyer I know! I bet she could help you learn!
Oh! That's a great idea!

Would you teach me how to fly, Nutmeg?

Of course! And actually . . . maybe we can all help you learn to control your magic?

That would be great!

We thanked the dragons and said good-bye.

On our way back to the **UNIPODS**, we talked about how we couldn't wait to help Charm. Tomorrow is going to be so fun!

5 The Unicorn Witch School

Thursday

Today, we were all excited to help Charm. We set up our very own Unicorn Witch School! But when it was time to get started, Charm didn't look happy.

Are you okay, Charm?
I feel bad that I need all this help.
Charm, everyone is good at different things! You might need some help with flying. But you don't need any help baking yummy treats!

Yeah, I'm terrible at mane styling. Nutmeg is much better than me!
But Piper is so much better at math than me!
I can't make people laugh like Sunny can.
But no one dances better than Bo!

We talked about what we were and weren't good at. And we realized we were <u>all</u> good at something!

The rest of the day was **GLITTERRIFIC** fun! We had made a sky obstacle course. Nutmeg showed Charm how to fly around it!

Charm flew through hoops and did many loop-the-loops! It was incredible! And Charm was really loving it!

At **CLOUDTIME**, we shared how our special Unicorn Powers work.

Oh, so why don't you think about yours?

I don't have a pet. Most witches have a cat. But I'm allergic to fur. It makes me sneeze. And sneezing makes me crash!

Then tomorrow, we will find you a non-sneezy new pet!

I really think this idea will work, Diary! What kind of animal do you think Charm should have as a pet?

6 A New Pet

Friday

This morning, Charm, Sunny, and I set out early to find Charm a pet. We visited Edna the gnome first because she always helps non-magical animals.

Do you know of any animals who need a special home?
They need to be furless and enjoy flying!
Why, yes, I do! And I see why you need one – you have made friends with a witch! Come with me.

Edna introduced Charm to a pigeon.

Charm gave a big smile. Maybe they could help each other fly!

Sunny and I could see there was a magic connection between the witch and the pigeon.

Gwendoline cooed back. Then Charm and Gwendoline flew up into the sky!

Later, we all met at the **UNIPODS**.

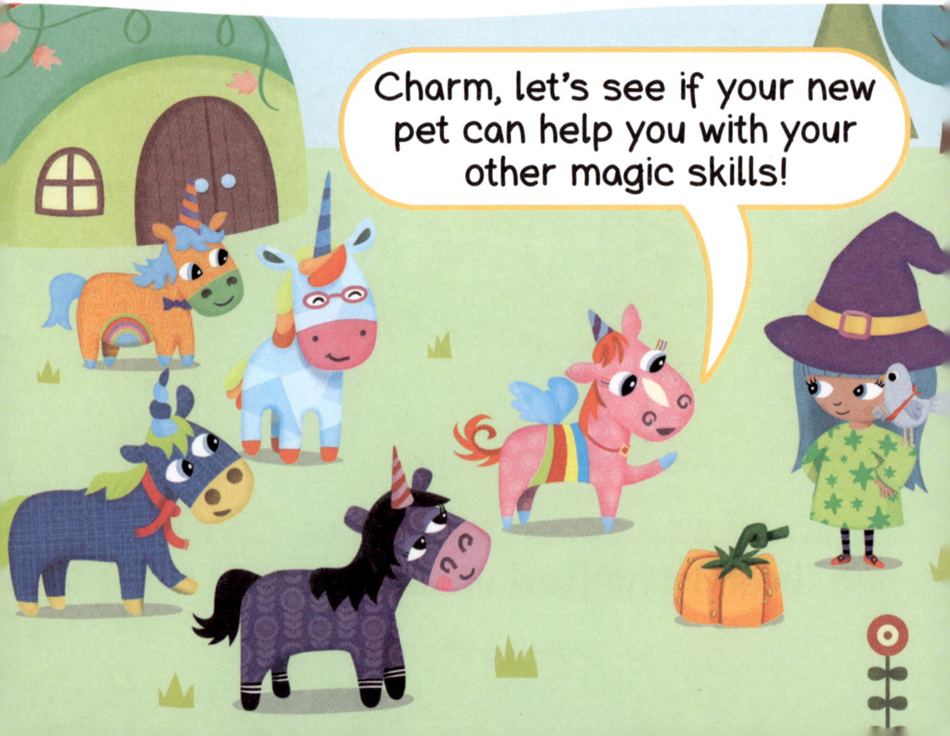

Charm, let's see if your new pet can help you with your other magic skills!

Charm took a deep breath. In fact, we all did!

PUMPKIN MOU-SEE-OH!

Yay!

Aww, he's so cute!

The pumpkin had turned into a mouse!

Charm handed the mouse to Nutmeg.

Maybe you could keep him. He could be your special pet!

Wow, thank you, Charm! I will name him Pumpkin!

We played with Pumpkin and Gwendoline until it was time for Charm to leave.

I learned how to fly and control my magic thanks to all of you. But the best thing I learned is that it's okay to be good at different things and to need help sometimes.

We all cheered. But we knew it was now time to say good-bye to Charm and Gwendoline. Then Mr. Rumptwinkle appeared with good news!

Guess what, unicorns!

You've all earned your Learning Patch! I will give out your patches during the Sparklegrove Patch Parade tomorrow. And I think Charm should stay for the parade!

So we asked Charm and Gwendoline to please stay one more night. And luckily, they agreed!

Before **CLOUDTIME**, we played bubble-pop together!

Oh, Diary! Tomorrow is going to be the best day ever!

7
The Patch Parade

Saturday

At breakfast this morning, Charm was busy baking up a storm. Gwendoline likes baking (or making messes), too!

Together, they made <u>loads</u> of yummy candy clouds, buttercup dreams, and **BUTTERFLUFF** cakes!

My classmates are going to be so amazed! I've gotten much more confident at flying and using my magic.

We're so glad to help. And thank you for making us all these treats!

You're very welcome, my friends!

Soon, it was time for the Patch Parade! Mr. Rumptwinkle gave us our Learning Patches. He even gave one to Charm!

Then, we partied! Charm used her magic to make even more yummy desserts! After lots of dancing and glitter, it was time for Charm and Gwendoline to go home.

It was sad to say good-bye. But we felt lucky to have created amazing memories with our new friend. We learned a lot about witches and how to help new friends.

We all gave Charm a big hug. Then, she and Gwendoline flew off up above the clouds. Charm promised she'd come back to visit.

I'm so glad we were able to meet a witch and help her, too!

Yeah, I'm also happy we're good at different things.

Me too – life would be very boring if we were all the same!

Of course, there is one thing we're both good at, though – sleeping!

What a **GLITTERRIFIC** week, Diary!
But for now, I gotta fly. See you next time!

Rebecca Elliott may not have a magical horn or sneeze glitter, but she's still a lot like a unicorn. Rebecca always tries to have a positive attitude, she likes to laugh a lot, and she lives with some great creatures — her noisy-yet-charming children, her lovable but naughty dog, Frida, and a big, lazy cat named Bernard. She gets to hang out with these fun characters and write stories for a living, so she thinks her life is pretty magical!

Rebecca is the author of several picture books, the young adult novel PRETTY FUNNY FOR A GIRL, the bestselling Unicorn Diaries early chapter book series, and the bestselling Owl Diaries series.

Unicorn Diaries

How much do you know about Bo and the Witch?

Bo and their friends are very excited to see a witch! Reread chapter 1. What are four fun facts about witches?

A witch named Charm crash-lands in Sparklegrove Forest. What happens to her broom? How do the unicorns decide to help?

In chapter 3, the unicorns are excited to help Charm make a new broom. What six materials do they need to find? What special item can help power a witch's broom?

In chapter 4, the unicorns help Charm practice her spells and learn how to fly. List all the different magical creatures Charm meets as she travels through the forest.

Reread page 56. How do witches make their magic happen? Then on page 58, who do Charm and the unicorns go to see for help and what is she able to offer?